Badminton
R U L E S

Badminton
R U L E S

PAT DAVIS

WARD LOCK

A WARD LOCK BOOK

First published in the UK 1998
by Ward Lock
Wellington House
125 Strand
LONDON WC2R 0BB

A Cassell Imprint

Distributed in the United States by
Sterling Publishing Co., Inc.
387 Park Avenue South,
New York, NY 10016–8810

**British Library Cataloguing-in-Publication
Data**
A catalogue record for this book is available
from the British Library

ISBN 0 7063 7734 6

Photographs by Peter Richardson

Printed and bound in Great Britain by Hillman
Printers (Frome) Ltd, Somerset

Frontispiece: Badminton is a get-up-and-go
sport as exemplified by this towering jump
smash.

CONTENTS

ACKNOWLEDGEMENTS

Very sincere thanks are due to the ever patient and ever helpful staff at the headquarters of the Badminton Association of England and of the International Badminton Federation. Thanks are also due to these organizations for permission to adapt illustrative material from their handbooks.

INTRODUCTION

Badminton, with its dancing footwork; its dashes around the court; its power smashes and contrastingly delicate drop shots; its lunges to take the shuttle mere inches from the floor; and its lightning reflex rallies mid-court, has attracted many millions of players throughout the world. Yet for all its athleticism and speed, badminton is easy to start.

Badminton's birthplace was Badminton House, the stately home of the 10th Duke of Beaufort, Master of the Queen's Horse. In its palatial entrance hall, badminton's forerunner, battledore and shuttlecock, was played by the Duke's seven daughters. As proof of this, long-handled, vellum-faced battledores may still be seen there. On one of them is written 'The Lady Henrietta Somerset, in February 1845, kept up with Miss Sybil Mitchell, 2018.' – a fantastic achievement for two young girls playing with a large 'cauliflower' shuttlecock!

The game grew from that simple beginning and on rainy days house guests turned it into a gently competitive sport. It was, however, a game without any real rules until John Lorraine Baldwin turned his mind to regulate it in about 1868. He was already the author of two books of rules for card games.

At about this time badminton was also played in India, in Poona and Karachi. In the latter the court, as at Badminton House, was pinched in at the middle by the posts so that double doors could be thrown open without disturbing posts or players. It became known as an hourglass court.

Baldwin's were the first of a plethora of rules for the new game. In 1876, J. Buchanan wrote 'Rules for the Anglo-Indian Game of Badminton or Lawn Rackets'. Two years later, H. Day, Racket Master at Kennington Oval, outdid tennis in his rules by giving the server no fewer than three attempts in which to hit the shuttle. In addition, he generously gave the non-serving

side the right at game-ball to choose their best player (probably one of four) to receive it! In the same year Julian Marshall's 'Lawn Tennis and Badminton devoted only two of its 60 pages to the latter.

In 1873 the first 'Poona Laws' came from India. These rules were later revised by J. H. E. Hunt three times and were also the basis on which Col. S. S. C. Dolby worked in 1893 when the Badminton Association (BA) was formed and the first official Laws of Badminton were written. These are the basis of the Laws followed today.

The BA originated in Southsea with just 14 south-coast clubs as sponsors. Over the next 40 years, a further 1,000 clubs were formed and joined the BA.

In 1934 Ireland, Scotland and Wales urged the formation of an international association which became known as the International Badminton Federation (IBF). The BA relegated itself to become the Badminton Association of England (BAE), one among nine founder members of the IBF, and gave full control of the game to the newly-formed body.

The IBF is now the worldwide law-maker and final arbiter on badminton matters. It controls the changing and updating of the Laws. Today it has no fewer than 160 member countries, ranging alphabetically from Argentina to Zimbabwe, and geographically from Iceland to New Zealand.

Many players never read the rules and simply pick them up as they go along. Too often they learn them incorrectly from others and so they may often have cheated, quite unwittingly, and thus gained distinct advantages. This is especially true of that vital first stroke, the service, which is governed by many complex rules.

It is up to all players to know the Laws of Badminton and when they are called upon to umpire, as even at club level they may well be asked to do, to implement them rigorously.

No doubt all players seek to play fairly. But, unless you know the Laws inside out, it is difficult to be your own judge and jury as to whether or not you are breaking them. It is certainly quite impossible for you as a player to see whether or not you are observing those all-important service laws (see pages 33–7). So ask a friend – a not too friendly friend – to vet you in play.

Most importantly, enjoy the following pages which can give you a clear conscience and a clean reputation as a knowledgeable, sporting badminton player.

The dancing footwork that is typical of badminton and is essential if a player is to change direction quickly and take the shuttle early – for a winner!

NOTE
Throughout the book, players and officials are referred to as 'he'. This is done purely for grammatical convenience, and is in no way intended to exclude women.

DRESS

● CLOTHING

Clothes do not make a good player, but a wise choice aids self-confidence as well as ensuring ease and comfort during a gruelling match.

What club players may wear is not prescribed by the Laws but there are regulations for top players in major events which must be strictly adhered to. These deal with designs, lettering and advertising on clothing in great detail and are inappropriate for inclusion in this book.

For rank and file club players the following points should be borne in mind when purchasing kit. It should be acceptable sports clothing and not too garish. Whilst colour is acceptable, it should not be taken to extreme lengths. For many years, 'all-white' was the order of the day for competition. Now it is 'predominantly white' with discreet stripes and blocks of colour permitted. Matching outfits for doubles partners are becoming popular. For non-competition games choice of clothing is largely a matter of personal preference.

Wise buys
Observing the following practical points will help to make play comfortable:

- blouses and shirts should be free-fitting but not too baggy and made of sweat-absorbing material
- shorts or skirts should not be tight and should be short enough to avoid any restriction of movement
- sweaters or cardigans not only help to keep players warm during long waits in cold halls but also play an important part in warming up and cooling down exercises (see pages 29–31)
- tracksuits will also keep you warm before and after a game but do not wear them on court during play as they will hamper your movement

- wristbands are invaluable for quick mopping up operations in a game which the Laws decree must be continuous
- headbands are useful to keep long hair and perspiration from blurring the vision at crucial moments

These are small points, but added together they can help make you a slightly better player.

This mixed doubles partnership shows typical dress for men and women on court for competition.

● FOOTWEAR

The wise player spends more time and money on his shoes than on his clothing. Shoes are the foundation of speed, and speed to and from the shuttle is your most potent weapon.

The Laws have plenty to say about foot-faults (see pages 35–7) but nothing on the choice of footwear. Shoes can look very attractive but in a game that demands constant stopping

and starting, twisting and turning, leaping and lungeing, it is even more important to ensure that they are:

- light and flexible enough for toe to be easily bent to heel
- snug but not so tight-fitting as to lead to abrasion
- laced right up the instep
- built up at the back to help support the Achilles tendon
- fitted with a cushioned inner sole to prevent jarring and eventual fatigue
- reinforced at the toe to obviate the effect of 'drag' when playing lunge-lobs
- sufficiently grooved and ridged along the sole to give essential grip on sometimes slippery wood floors

A wise player also carries with him a second pair of shoes with a smoother sole for use on a tacky surface. Make sure that before you buy any shoes you try them on with the same type of socks that you will wear for play. Some clubs dislike the use of black-soled shoes on wood floors and do not allow them on court.

A careful choice of footwear can make you faster on to the shuttle and leave you fresher and faster for vital last points.

● COURT-SIDE BAG

Top players can be seen placing huge sports bags, bristling with a battery of spare rackets, by the side of the court. This is permitted, provided that it creates no distraction, and to speed up any necessary resort to it, it is moved with the player whenever he changes ends. In a game in which the Laws demand continuous play and delays and departures from court are discouraged, all players would do well to follow their example . . . a little more modestly perhaps. This time-saving bag should contain:

- spare shoe-laces
- a small towel
- glucose tablets
- safety pins
- glasses demister, if needed
- a spare racket of exactly the same weight, feel, tension and balance as the one you are using
- a second pair of shoes with alternative soles
- a few new shuttles for knock-up practice (see page 29), of the correct speed for the hall you are playing in

This lucky dip of a bag should have its various items readily available. A strict umpire will not tolerate a long search for a submerged safety pin!

EQUIPMENT

● RACKETS

Badminton rackets weigh roughly a mere 98g (3½oz): rather less than a modest bar of chocolate! The joy of this is that they can be wielded without difficulty by children and veterans alike. The very lightness of the racket makes badminton a fast reflex game in which deception can also be effectively employed with a last-second change of racket pace and direction.

Law 5 lays down stringent regulations as to the racket's vital statistics:

- the frame shall not be longer than 680mm (2ft 2¼in) or wider than 230mm (9in)
- the stringed area shall be of crossed strings alternately interlaced where they cross. It shall be of uniform pattern, not less dense in the centre than in any other area

- the stringed area shall not exceed 280mm (11in) in overall length and 220mm (8⅝in) in overall width

Choice of racket

When you are choosing a racket, the manufacturer will certainly have adhered to the dimensions above, so it is much more important to consider the following points:

- handle circumferences vary between 80mm (3¼in) and 95mm (3¾in). Make sure you choose one that is neither too small nor too large or you may suffer muscle strain or lose a firm grip on the racket. A small handle can always be built up with an extra towelling grip which will also help those with damp palms
- for general use it should have a spiralled, overlapping leather grip
- the shaft should have flexibility or 'whip' for added power. To test this, hold the racket horizontally and

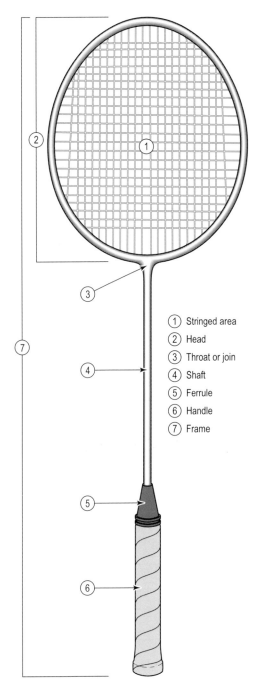

1. Stringed area
2. Head
3. Throat or join
4. Shaft
5. Ferrule
6. Handle
7. Frame

The sections of a badminton racket.

press gently upwards with the thumbs on head and handle. You should see a slight curvature of the shaft

- to prevent abrasion the strings should run in channels where they are threaded round the head, and the stringing holes should be lined with plastic grommets
- the strings themselves should be of white, transparent natural gut or a fine synthetic gut, strung at a tension of about 7kg (15lb) pressure
- natural gut has more kick-back than a synthetic one but it loses tension if it becomes damp, wears out more quickly, and is more expensive. For all that, for both power and touch, natural gut is best
- the head should have the largest possible 'sweet spot', the stringed area giving the maximum resilience and therefore power
- as a good test of the racket's tautness, a fingernail flicked across the strings should emit a sharp, clear note and the mesh should yield only fractionally to pressure of the thumbs
- the racket should be well balanced, roughly 60mm (2⅜in) from the throat and should be neither head- nor handle-heavy
- the racket should be made of graphite, boron, ceramic, or a mixture of all three to give both strength and lightness
- prices for a worthwhile racket vary quite widely – buy the best you can afford!

● SHUTTLECOCKS

No other sport has so light a missile: five shuttlecocks weigh only 28g (1oz)! Yet it can be struck repeatedly and hard to leave the racket at well over 160kmph (100mph). It is a miniature aerodynamic marvel! Its design must be as follows:

- the shuttle shall have 16 feathers (generally white and from the same wing of a goose) fixed in the base
- the base shall be rounded, 25–28mm (1–1⅛in) in diameter
- the feathers may be 62–70mm (2½–2¾in) in overall length but must be of exactly similar length from base to tip
- these tips must form a circle with a diameter of 58–68mm (2¼–2⅝in)
- the feathers must be reinforced with interwoven thread round the quills in order to maintain the above spread
- it shall weigh from 4.74–5.50g (73–85 grains)

Shuttle speed
A shuttle's 'speed' is actually the distance it will travel. This depends on three things: the shuttle's weight, the spread of the feathers and the atmosphere through which it flies.

The heavier the weight, up to a certain limit, the faster and further a shuttle will fly. Conversely, the wider the spread of the feathers (as with a

parachute) the more slowly it will travel. So in a large hall holding a big volume of cold, dense air, a shuttle will fly a shorter distance than in a small, well-heated hall where the air resistance is lessened.

There is therefore a suitable shuttle for different halls at different temperatures. Feathered shuttles are made with the same spread of feathers but are of differing weights, numerically graded from 73 to 85. These figures indicate the weight in grains (1 grain = 0.065g) and therefore the speed. Numbers 73–75 are regarded as 'slow'; 76–77 as 'slow medium'; 78–81 as 'medium'; 82–83 as 'fast medium'; 84–85 as 'fast'.

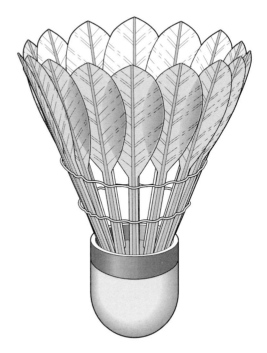

A feathered shuttle.

As a rough guide, 76–77 would be suitable for a very small, warm, one-court hall; 78–79 for a rather larger hall; 80–82 for a big hall with two or three courts; 83–84 only for an exceptionally large, lofty and cold hall. Much depends on the temperature. At the extreme, shuttles much slower than 73 are made for use in high altitude locations like Johannesburg where, at 1,524m (5,000ft), the air is much thinner than at sea level.

Shuttle testing

To test whether a shuttle is of the correct speed, it must be held so that it is exactly above the back boundary line. It should be hit with a full stroke on a rising trajectory parallel to the sidelines. If it falls in the area delineated by the two sideline markers near the back of the court it is the correct speed for that hall. If it falls beyond the back marker, it is too fast; short of the front one, it is too slow.

Shuttle care

The shuttlecock is delicate and expensive so treat it with care. Make sure you do not:

- bang tubes on the floor to open them
- store them near dry heat, or their quills will lose their natural oil and become brittle
- store them high up (hot air rises) or low down on damp floors

- use shuttles that are too slow for the court or you will quickly wear them out
- scoop them back under the net or hit them on the half-volley as they land – both cause damage
- thrust them back into the tube feathers first
- roughly tear them apart if their glued, reinforced threads cause them to stick together
- forget to smooth ruffled feathers between thumb and forefinger

Loving care means longer life and longer life means less expense!

A synthetic shuttle.

Synthetic shuttles

Shuttles may also be made of synthetic material. They are very similar in appearance to feathered shuttles but their 'skirts' are made of perforated plastic, not feathers. Their flight characteristics should be roughly similar to those of a natural-feathered shuttle. They are often manufactured with a yellow or gold skirt to make them more clearly visible and are colour-graded 'slow', 'medium' and 'fast'.

They are, however, seldom used in top-flight play. Expert players cannot accustom themselves, in a game demanding absolute accuracy, to their rather different flight, turnover, and feel on the racket. More durable and slightly cheaper on the whole, they are extensively used by players at club level.

COURT ETIQUETTE

Etiquette depends on courtesy and goodwill rather than on rules. It is the oil that makes games run more smoothly and sweetly. These guidelines are the unwritten laws of badminton. Flout them and you will lose no points – just the esteem of your partner and other players. Observe them and you will become a popular player, in demand as a partner.

Some points are simple common sense or ordinary good manners. Others, for a beginner, may need a little explanation. Know them well so that in the heat of the game, they do not slip your mind. It is good practice to:

- briefly congratulate, cheer, consult or commiserate with your doubles partner during play
- after club games thank your partner and opponents; after league or county matches, shake hands – not forgetting the umpire
- treat shuttles with respect – hand rather than throw them to your partner
- wear clean and correct kit
- be as punctual for club play as for tournaments and matches
- if you are sure of a line decision say so; if in a little doubt give it against yourself; if in great doubt ask for a 'let' to be played
- volunteer to keep the score in club games
- avoid both gamesmanship and showmanship

It is considered bad practice to:

- walk behind or across another court while a rally is in progress
- 'poach' your partner's shots because you are sure you can play them better than he can! For your partner it is demoralizing and can leave you way out of position

After a mixed doubles match, international players shake hands at the net.

- leave your opponent to retrieve a shuttle which you have hit into the net
- return a fallen shuttle to your opponent by scooping it under the net. Throw or hit it back accurately
- shout noisily or distractingly during play
- query the umpire's or the linesman's decision by look or gesture. If it is about a vital point on which you are certain he has erred, query it politely, and gracefully accept his ruling, even if it is against you
- make line decisions for your opponents on their side of the net: these are solely their responsibility
- leave a tournament without thanking the referee and behind-the-scenes workers for their efforts
- batter, bounce or throw the racket in bad temper
- alter a shuttle's speed, covertly, by turning over the tips of the feathers without the consent of your opponents or the umpire. Besides, it is against the Laws of Badminton
- leave the hall during a tournament without the referee's permission
- change the shuttle unnecessarily in tournaments and certainly not without consulting your opponents. If you and your opponents disagree about the correct flight or speed of a shuttle, the umpire's decision on the matter is final

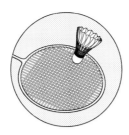

HALLS AND COURTS

Until fairly recently, when sports centres mushroomed in every town, badminton was played in a wide variety of buildings. They were often too small to accommodate the regulation-size court – 13.40m (44ft) long and 6.10m (20ft) wide. Enthusiastic clubs with little alternative accommodation available manfully put up with such difficulties. With low ceilings and obstructions like structural beams, fluorescent lights and even gas heaters, 'local rules' often had to be framed. Generally, hitting the roof was ruled to be a fault, since a player in difficulties could do so deliberately. Hitting other impediments was felt to warrant a 'let'.

 ## THE HALL

The dimensions of the ideal hall as recommended by the BAE (and dreamed of by run-of-the-mill club players) are as follows:

- at international level there must be a clear height of 9.15m (30ft) above the court; at club level this is reduced to 7.6m (25ft)
- there should be clear space round the court: a minimum of 1.52m (5ft) at each end; 1.22m (4ft) at the sides; and .91m (3ft) between parallel courts

Background
Badminton has long been bedevilled not only by poor lighting but also by poor shuttle visibility. The BAE has therefore laid down its own recommendations to improve both of these. End walls should be of a dark

colour, preferably green with a matt finish to prevent glare. They should not contain windows.

Artificial lighting

Not less than 2kW of lighting per court are essential either in the form of:

- 5 x 200kW lamps on each side, or
- twin 1.524m (5ft) fluorescent tubes mounted end to end. These should be .91m (3ft) outside the sidelines, centred on the net and some 5m (16ft) above the floor
- all lights should be enclosed or shielded to keep glare to a minimum

● THE COURT

For doubles, this is a long, narrow rectangle measuring 13.40m (44ft) long and 6.1m (20ft) wide. For singles, it is of course smaller – still 13.40m (44ft) in length but now only 5.180m (17ft) in width. It is advisable to learn the names of the various lines and

Men's doubles action from the All England Championships shows the amount of space around the court, clear court markings and a taut, well-secured net on the sideline. Perfect playing conditions!

areas of the court, and also to note that a cross-court clear has to be hit considerably harder and further than a straight one!

The area from the net to the short service line is known as the 'forecourt'; from the short service line to, roughly, the doubles long service line as the 'mid-court'; the remainder

to the back boundary line is called the 'rear court'.

In doubles, the spaces between the parallel sidelines and between the parallel doubles long service line and the back boundary line are known as 'tramlines'. The spaces in the rear court in the corners between the sidelines are the 'back boxes'.

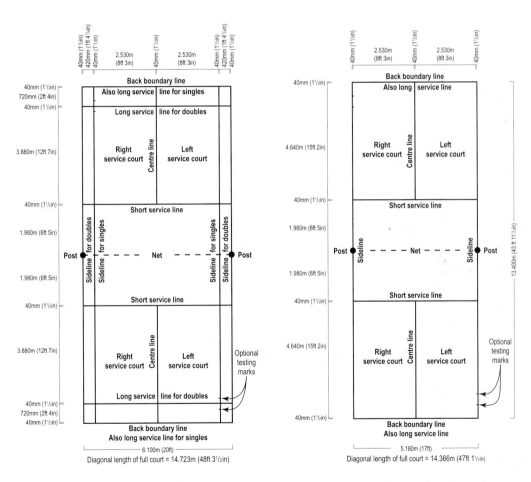

A court which is marked out for both singles and doubles play.

A court marked out for singles play only.

Surfaces

In tennis, play on grass, clay, artificial surfaces or wood radically alters the game. This of course is not the case in badminton, which is a purely volleying game. On striking the floor the shuttle is dead. The composition of the floor can, however, make a difference to footwork.

The ideal floor is probably of sprung maple – provided it is neither slippery nor reflective. It looks attractive and is very easy on the feet, even giving them a slight impetus. Much more common are concrete or composition floors. The former are hard on both feet and shoes. The latter, level and non-slip, are most commonly used.

The Hova court (named after its inventor, the Borough Surveyor of Hove) is ideal but expensive. It is a green, cushion-backed, non-slip PVC floor covering that has all the necessary lines marked on it. In two parts, it can be laid and taken up comparatively quickly. It is secured to the underlying floor by broad adhesive strips. Because of its attractive appearance and non-slip qualities it is used for many major events with IBF approval.

Whatever the surface, Law 1 decrees that the lines on it be distinctly marked out 40mm (1½in) wide, preferably in white or yellow. These lines form part of the court they define.

To show the area into which a shuttle of correct speed should fall when tested (see page 16), two marks 40 x 40mm (1½ x 1½in) are made inside the singles line, 530m (1ft 9in) and

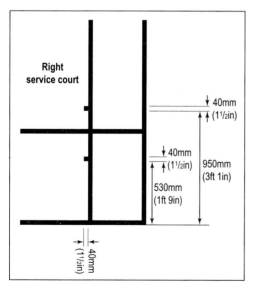

The marks for testing shuttle speed as they would be shown on a doubles court.

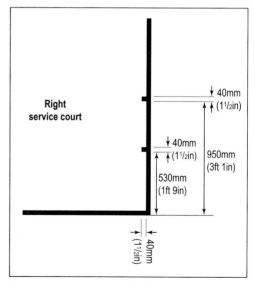

The marks for testing shuttle speed in position on a singles court.

950m (3ft 1in) respectively from the back boundary line.

Posts

These should stand 1.55m (5ft 1in) in height from the surface of the court. They must be placed on the doubles sidelines for singles as well as for doubles. They must also be sufficiently firm to take the necessary tension when the net is strained across them to its full height.

There should be no gap between the post and the net through which a shuttle could pass. This can be ensured by the use of hooks down the inside of the posts and a draw-cord along the bottom of the net.

Net

At all times this should be tightly strained so that its height from the floor is 1.524m (5ft) in the centre, and 1.55m (5ft 1in) at the posts.

A measuring rod, 1.524m (5ft) long, should be kept by the umpire's chair to facilitate regular testing to ensure that the net is still at its correct central height and has not sagged. Too often, at club level, players congregate at the net to discuss a point and unthinkingly pull it down to see over it – a steadily sagging net results. The following regulations govern the type and size of net:

• it should be woven of a fine, dark cord and be of an even mesh, not less than 15mm (⅝in) and not more than 20mm (¾in). Nylon nets have the disadvantage that when shuttles have to be disentangled from them the feathers' plumes can be damaged
• it should be 760mm (2½ft) deep and at least 6.1m (20ft) wide
• along its top the net should be clearly edged with white tape, doubled over to a depth of 75mm (3in) on each side with the draw-cord running through it

SCORING

Many beginners find badminton scoring difficult to pick up. This may be because they are already accustomed to tennis's very different system, acquired by actually playing or by hearing it repeatedly on television. Without tennis's 'deuce' and 'advantage', it is basically simple. It does however use 'love' as a term for '0'. An understanding of the system depends on realizing the two following basic points:

- a point can be gained only when a rally is won by the server in singles, or by one of the serving side in doubles
- after each rally won, the server continues to serve but from the other service court on his side of the net

● SINGLES

Having won the toss or spin, player A elects to serve first, and must do so from the right-hand service court.

As long as A wins rallies, he scores points and changes sides for each serve: 1–0, 2–0, 3–0. When he loses a rally, the serve passes to player B, his opponent, with the score at 0–3, who serves as above until he also loses a rally. Then the serve reverts back to A, at 3–0 perhaps if B has failed to add to his score. On these reversions the server serves from the right service court if his score is even: 0, 2, 4, 6, etc., and from the left service court if his score is odd: 1, 3, 5, etc. The server's score is always called first.

● DOUBLES

Scoring in doubles is basically the same as in singles. Player A, partnered by B, elects to serve first and must do so from the right-hand service court. When a rally is lost, the serve passes, not to an opponent (X or Y) but to his partner, B. B serves, winning points and changing sides at each service until a second rally, and with it the second service, is lost. Service now passes to opponents X and Y, with X serving first from the right-hand service court. When they in turn have lost two rallies, the service reverts to A and B. Whenever service is thus regained it commences from the right-hand service court.

The only slight quirk is that, at the very outset of the game, the pair serving first have only one serve, not two. Note also that when the second partner begins to serve, 'second server' must be called after the score; for example, '6–2, second server'. This obviates any likelihood of argument when a further rally is lost.

● SETTING

In badminton there are no tie-breaks as such. There is, however, a slight complication if the scores reach 14–all. Then the first side to reach 14 has two options:

- either to 'play straight through', i.e. to play up to 15 as usual, or
- 'to set', i.e. to revert 14–all to love–all and then play on until one side scores 3 extra points, for example 3–2. In this case the official score will be shown as 17–15.

Ladies' singles are played up to 11 points; setting is at 10–all to 13 points.

On busy evenings most games, for a quick turn round, are only a single game up to 15 points. If a slightly longer game is preferred, it is permissible to play up to 21. In club matches and championships, play is almost invariably the best of three games of 15. The player or pair winning a game starts serving in the next one.

● CHANGING ENDS

In order that opposing players or pairs have roughly the same time at each end (one sometimes has much better background visibility than the other) they are changed as follows:

- in a single game up to 15, when the first player or pair has scored 8. In one up to 11, at a score of 6
- in a game up to 21, when the first player or pair has scored 11
- in a three-game match, after the first and second games, and at a score of 8 in the third

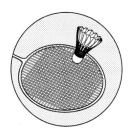

BEFORE THE GAME

It is just as well to realize from the outset that badminton is a get-up-and-go kind of game. There are no brief rests after every second game as in tennis and no breaks between 'halves' as in professional soccer. Badminton is virtually a non-stop game.

● CONTINUOUS PLAY

Law 18.1 is quite adamant on this point: play must be continuous from the first serve to the end of the match.

Although not all countries are as hot and humid as Malaysia and Indonesia, where sweat has been known to run down into a player's shoes, a 90-second interval is permitted between the first and second sets; one of five minutes between the second and third sets in:

- competitive international events
- IBF-sanctioned events
- other matches, unless, as the BAE has done, a member association prefers not to implement this, except in international matches

Only in the latter break may the court be left without the umpire's permission. Coaching is allowed only in these intervals. Apart from these breaks, play must not be suspended for the player to regain his breath or strength, receive coaching, or have a 'comfort break'. Nor may he leave the court without the umpire's permission. Any player who deliberately holds up play by repeatedly tying shoelaces, towelling down, demisting spectacles, and so on may first be warned, then faulted, and finally reported to the referee who is empowered to disqualify him.

In the case of injury or illness, only the referee, and doctor or paramedic may come on court to help assess the situation. Thereafter, the decision as to how much respite a player may be given is solely in the hands of the umpire. Equally he must also see that the player's opponent is in no way put at a disadvantage by getting cold or stiff, or by losing rhythm or concentration.

● THE KNOCK-UP

With such a 'get-up-and-get-on-with-it' philosophy it is hardly surprising that only a bare three minutes is allowed for the customary pre-match, on-court knock-up for adults and a mere two for juniors.

In view of this, wise use must be made of every second allowed by the IBF. So be on court, ready for action, as soon as allowed by the match captain, umpire or referee. For the full three minutes be on your toes, concentrating one hundred per cent.

For this preliminary preparation, so that you immediately find your touch, do not use the battered shuttles from the previous match. Instead make use of three or four of the shuttles of correct speed for the hall, that you wisely carry in your court-side bag (see page 12).

Now, for doubles, put into practice a series of complementary strokes that you have already rehearsed, for example:

- hit a high, perfect-length doubles serve which your partner returns with a smash to the body. Return this with a flat push that he lobs, so that you in your turn can smash to his body and so on
- similarly, hit a high service to the back boundary line from which your partner can play a drop-shot so that you can make a net-return. This he returns with a similarly tight shot, forcing you to lob so that the drop-shot, net-return routine continues. Then change roles
- play a rally of backhand overhead (or round the head) clears for length – and recovery
- above all, leave time for the often neglected low serve: the most important stroke in your doubles armoury
- leave time too for the almost equally neglected and equally important net-return of service and the subsequent rally of tight net-shots

To crowd all these strokes without undue hurry into a bare three minutes before the umpire calls 'Time!' needs rehearsal.

● PHYSICAL WARM-UP

Though the actual knock-up on court is restricted to three minutes, the IBF imposes no time limit on the equally vital, but often neglected, preceding warm-up in the dressing-room.

After a light meal, arrive unhurriedly an hour before play to warm up. In particular concentrate on getting supple by doing some bending and stretching exercises such as sideways body bends; neck rolls; shoulder and triceps stretches; back and hip turns; foot and ankle rotations; hamstring stretches and lunges. Keep the time lapse between exercising and playing to a minimum.

These exercises ensure that the danger of strained and torn muscles is greatly reduced, and that your flexibility for ease of stroke and greater reach is increased. They should in no way leave you feeling jaded – rather the reverse. All can be completed within twenty minutes. Light skipping also will help create instant mobility. Once warmed up in this way, keep your tracksuit on until called on to court. You should cool off in a similar way to avoid stiffness.

● MENTAL WARM-UP

Doubles partners are not allowed time for mid-game tactical consultations so a pre-match mental warm-up is vital – as it is for the singles player. Refer to your memory, or to a 'diary of opponents', kept from previous encounters or observation, which lists weaknesses for attack; strengths to avoid; and favourite shots and reflex returns to anticipate.

Bearing in mind your own qualities and defects, plan the strokes and tactics that you will seek to impose on your opponent. Also have in mind details of changes of strategy and tactics should those first thought of fail to work.

When you step on court be just as fully tuned mentally as physically. Well-merited confidence, but not over-confidence, breeds success.

● TOSSING UP

This used to be done by spinning the racket, calling 'rough' or 'smooth' and then feeling the 'trebling' at the bottom of the head. These slender, coloured strings were inter-woven through the verticals to keep them from bunching or spreading. One side felt distinctly rough; the other, smooth.

With more efficient modern stringing, trebling disappeared. Players now have to make do with the manufacturer's or the racket's name, or

A pre-match physical warm-up will give you the suppleness, speed and reach to play strokes such as this difficult overhead clear.

the logo on the shaft, frame or ferrule. Alternatively, the players can resort to the more prosaic toss of a coin, 'heads' or 'tails'.

Laws 8.1 and 8.2 give the winner the choice of three options:

- to serve first
- to receive first
- to start play on their preferred end of the court

Most players choose to serve first, hoping to score a few early points to give them a reassuring lead. Others, especially if they are lethal receivers, do the opposite. Doubles partners, knowing that their opponents have only one serve initially, might hope to gain a first-strike winner and then, with two serves, run up a good lead.

Where one end of the court is much better, generally from the point of view of visibility, most players choose that first in the hope of winning the morale-boosting first game. Others, anticipating a close three-game match, are prepared to start at the worst end in order to play the last vital points at the best end.

● POST-MORTEM

After the game this is just as advisable as pre-match planning. If you won, notice if any particular strokes or tactics contributed to that victory. If you lost, do not get depressed: make sure that weak strokes, tactics and techniques are noted for further practice; that a new opponent is added to the diary; or that a resurgent old one is re-evaluated. In particular check on your own partnership in doubles. Were there gaps or clashes? Did you 'gel' both in play and personality? With thought and practice future victories can arise from defeat.

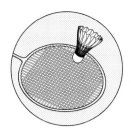

FAULTS IN PLAY

● SERVICE

It may appear strange that two of the great racket games should have such entirely different service strokes. In tennis, the server throws the ball high above his head and then hits it downwards steeply and with great power at 209kmph (130mph). In complete contrast, in badminton the shuttle is first dropped down and then, most frequently, hit slightly upwards at a steady 16kmph (10mph)! In both cases the service is of prime importance. Its effectiveness may determine the outcome, not merely of the game, but of the match itself.

The badminton service is dictated by the height of the net, a towering 1.524m (5ft); and by the distance of the point of impact from the net, between 1.524m (5ft) on a backhand serve and some 2.15m (7ft) on a forehand one.

How to play a low serve
In order to avoid faults, it is important to know the basics of a correct service:

- stand near the central T-junction, left foot pointing to the court diagonally opposite but right foot carrying most of the weight
- hold the shuttle by the tip of the feathers at about chest height; the racket in the basic grip, with both forearm and wrist bent well backwards, just to the side of the right thigh
- look at the tape, then at the target area which is about 300mm (1ft) behind the front service line, near the T-junction, so allowing a margin for error
- as the shuttle is dropped vertically down, just to the right of the front foot, sway the body-weight forward and push the racket smoothly at the shuttle, with the wrist bent back throughout, and eyes kept on the shuttle

- continuing the stroke smoothly to waist height, advance to the net, to intercept a net-return, with the racket now lifted to tape height

To avoid being 'killed' the shuttle should just skim the net on a final downward trajectory. Be unhurried, relaxed and confident.

There are, of course, a wide variety of other services such as the flick, drive, backhand and high. The low serve is explained here in detail because it is the most frequently used (except perhaps in singles) and is important. It clearly exemplifies the many possible breaches of the Laws which apply equally to other types of service.

Service faults

To ensure that the service is upwards, it is hedged about with more laws than any other stroke. Know all seven of the laws and you may well be the only club member who does!

The shuttle must be hit diagonally, underhand, to pass over the net and, if left to fall, land within the opposite service court's boundary. This includes

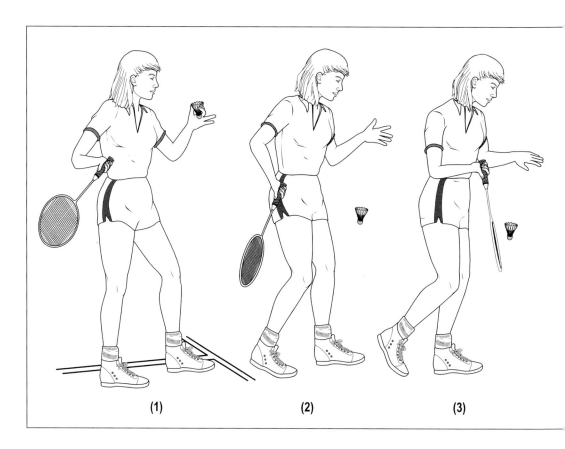

(1)   (2)   (3)

the lines which are therefore 'in'. At impact with the shuttle:

- the racket must be pointing downwards and the whole of the racket head must be clearly below the lowest part of the hand holding it
- the *whole* of the shuttle must be below the server's waist, i.e. an imaginary line round the body, level with the lowest part of the server's bottom rib
- both feet, or part of both feet, must be stationary throughout and in contact with the floor. They must

also be within the server's service court. Here even a toe on the line is a fault

- the service commences with the first forward movement of the racket. This must continue without pause, hesitation or backward movement in one continuous forward stroke. It is however within the Law to speed up the motion of the racket, or to slow it down, or to alter the angle of the racket head as in a flick, reverse flick or drive serve; always provided of course that it is a *continuous* stroke

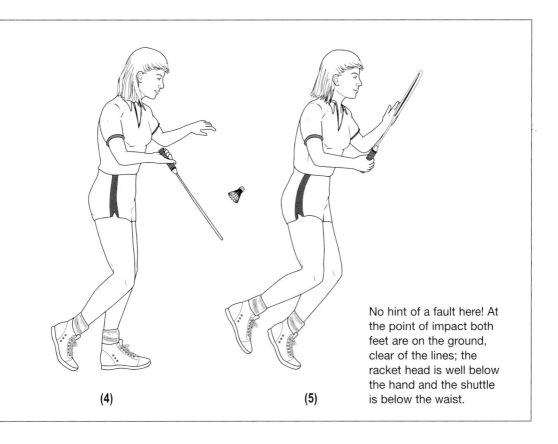

(4) (5)

No hint of a fault here! At the point of impact both feet are on the ground, clear of the lines; the racket head is well below the hand and the shuttle is below the waist.

- there must be no undue delay either in moving to the serving position or in the actual delivery of the serve. This is sometimes done, illegally, to enable the server, or his partner, to regain their composure or breath.
- on the other hand the server must not serve too quickly, i.e. before the receiver is ready. If he does so and

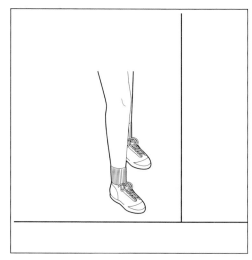

The correct position of the feet for serving, with both of them on the ground and well clear of the service and centre lines.

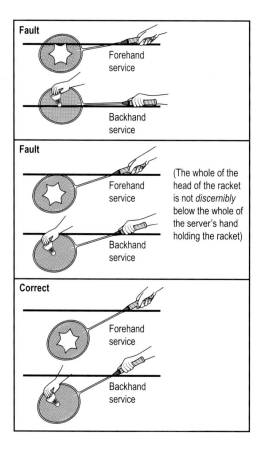

Fault

Forehand service

Backhand service

Fault

Forehand service

(The whole of the head of the racket is not *discernibly* below the whole of the server's hand holding the racket)

Backhand service

Correct

Forehand service

Backhand service

This diagram demonstrates two faulty services and a correct one for both forehand and backhand. It shows the levels of hand and racket at the point of striking the shuttle.

the receiver makes no move or action to return the shuttle, a 'let' is played. The Law, however, makes no stipulation as to how long is 'undue delay'. Any coach worth his salt will have emphasized 'Don't hurry your serve or you'll make an error.' So the happy medium between haste and delay is probably about ten seconds from the moment you move into your serving position to actual delivery

- it is a fault if the server completely misses the shuttle
- the racket must initially hit the base of the shuttle – not the feathers

The last point is an apparently strange law, for who in his senses would want

A common service fault with the front foot touching both centre and service lines. Get into the habit of checking the position of your feet before you start to concentrate on your service action.

to hit yielding feathers rather than a firm base? In the 1920s English international Hazel Hogarth did – and quite effectively too! It was not until the 1970s that Malaysian brothers, Misbun and Jalani Sidek, again hit the shuttle, held upside down, backhanded, slicing crisply across the feathers. The shuttle did everything except loop the loop: it swerved, twisted and dipped, forcing the receiver to play an upward lob rather than the customary net-shot, flat push or downward dab.

As a result, rallies became shorter and therefore less exciting. As the feathers had to be crisp for strokes to take full effect, steadily growing numbers of expensive shuttles were used. So this practice was banned by the IBF for the good of the game in general and for the sake of club coffers in particular.

Receiving faults

To maintain the balance between server and receiver the latter must also observe some restrictions, though not such stringent ones. He must:

- stand within the boundaries of his service court, i.e. a foot must not even touch a line
- keep both feet, or part of them, in contact with the floor
- remain stationary until the server actually strikes the shuttle. (To enforce this the umpire must be able to see service impact and receiver's initial movement simultaneously)

Here, with one foot off the ground, the server is at fault. At least part of both feet must be in contact with the floor when serving.

• refrain from distracting his opponent by growl, grimace, or racket-waving

In the unlikely event of receiver and server being faulted at the same time, a 'let' is played.

The receiver naturally does everything he can legally to 'threaten' the server: by standing right up to the front service line; by adopting a crouching stance on the balls of his feet; by holding his racket 'menacingly' forward, high or just above tape level. All these are perfectly legitimate ploys but they must not be exaggerated by unnecessary bouncing or racket-shaking.

Service court errors

A service court error occurs when a player serves out of turn or serves from the wrong service court. If the error is noticed before the next service is played, it is a 'let' and the service is replayed correctly – unless only one side is at fault and loses the rally. If the error is not noticed before the next service is played, the error should not be corrected.

Top players, especially when serving backhanded, hold the shuttle only inches below their waist to obtain the flattest possible trajectory.

● GENERAL PLAY

The shuttle is in play as soon as it is struck by the server. If it is a good serve, likely to fall in court, the receiver tries to return it over the net and within the confines of the opponent's court. If it falls short, the receiver does not play it and wins the rally.

In doubles this return may be played to either of the opponents;

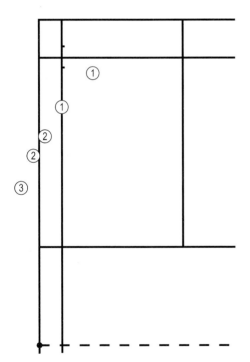

In this diagram for doubles, only the shuttle in position 3 is out. A shuttle that lands on either side of the court boundary line is considered to be in as long as it is touching the line.

either of whom may return it to either of their opponents. This sequence of strokes (a rally) continues until one of the four players makes a fault and a point is won or a service lost (see page 27).

General faults

There is a wide variety of faults, other than those made in serving or receiving, of which the complete player should be aware. Where they are not obvious, the player concerned should call 'fault' and explain what the fault was. It is obviously a fault if the shuttle:

- lands outside the court boundaries
- passes through, under or round the net
- fails to reach the net, or to pass over it
- touches the roof, ceiling or side walls (see page 21)

Faults near the net

These often occur in the cramped confines of the forecourt in very close proximity to the net. It is a fault if a player:

- touches the net or posts, no matter how gently, with his person, clothing or racket
- reaches over the net to intercept the shuttle before it crosses the net. It is, however, legal to follow through over the net provided the shuttle was first struck on the striker's side, and provided that

such a follow-through does not impede the opponent's next stroke
- hampers an opponent by following through across the net legitimately as above
- invades his opponent's court by inadvertently releasing his grip and so throwing his racket under or over the net; or by slipping and then sliding under the net himself, even without touching it
- baulks an opponent from making a net-return by waving his racket at random. He may however attempt a deliberate stroke to intercept the shuttle or defend his face

Other faults
It is also a fault if:

- the shuttle is caught and held on the racket, even momentarily, i.e. if it is slung, rather than hit with one clean stroke
- the shuttle is hit twice in succession by the same player in a single stroke. This may occur, for example,

Preparing to receive service in men's doubles. Note how the player about to receive is standing with his front foot just clear of the service line, and his back foot in contact with the floor.

in a tentative net-shot, a nervous low serve, or when desperately returning a smash if, immediately after initial contact, the racket involuntarily judders forward again to make a second contact

- the shuttle has first touched, no matter how lightly, the racket, hair, clothing or person of either player, more particularly of the non-striker
- if the shuttle's speed is deliberately altered by reducing or extending its spread, without umpire's or opponent's permission
- if a player distracts another by rowdy play (shouting, racket-waving, racket-throwing or making gestures). It is not a fault if one doubles partner shouts to the other, to assist him in judging shuttle-fall, by calling 'Leave!', 'Take!', or 'Watch!'
- if a player flagrantly and persistently prevents continuous play

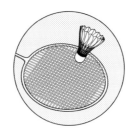

COURT OFFICIALS

To enforce the Laws of Badminton in top-class play, we need referees and umpires, service judges and linesmen. Even at lower levels, umpires at least are needed for club tournaments and sometimes for club matches.

Officials need not themselves have been top-ranking players who have experienced the high-level game they control. Many are older players, easing themselves out of the rigours of competitive play and looking for a useful and enjoyable badminton future which will keep them in touch with the game. All have attended special training courses and been examined and graded.

● THE REFEREE

The referee is not truly an on-court official. Much of his invaluable work, while not actually behind the scenes, is certainly done out of the limelight. He sits in sight of courts but not too near them. He is the overall controller of the tournament: the man or woman who works players smoothly and thoughtfully through four or five rounds to a grand final. He may also supervise a long rota of linesmen, service judges and umpires. When a tournament is a major, five- or six-court affair, he will certainly have assistant managers to take on these duties. If an umpire needs added authority – a final ruling on a tricky point, or help in dealing with an unsatisfied appeal by a player – the referee will actually come down 'on court'. At all times he is the final arbiter on the Laws though not necessarily on the actual events of a game.

● THE UMPIRE

The umpire, 'the man in the high chair', is the leader of a very necessary team and takes the brunt of the work. With so much responsibility in his hands – the winning or loss of a national championship for example – he must be a man of many qualities. He must have a strong voice, even in this tannoy age; quiet authority; a great enthusiasm for the game; and an encyclopaedic knowledge of the Laws.

The umpire must be meticulous in dress. The BAE dress code for men is navy blue or black blazer, plain grey trousers, matching socks and shoes, unpatterned pastel or white shirt and the official association tie. The ladies wear navy blue, black or grey jacket, grey skirt or trousers and plain pastel or white blouses.

Linesmen generally wear roughly the same as the umpire except that a one-colour sweater, often red, replaces the blazer.

This ladies' doubles match shows the umpire, service judge and four of the ten linesmen in position. In tournaments, such dedicated officials far outnumber the players.

Before play

Before there is a player in sight, the umpire has detailed duties to perform. The score pad has to be obtained from the referee; linesmen and service judges have to be briefed and ordered for the march on to court so that each one can break away at his appointed chair without disrupting the opening ceremony.

Once on court he must note the time on his score had and check that:

- tannoy and scoreboards are working
- posts are squarely on the sidelines
- the net is precisely 1.524m (5ft) high at the centre with no gaps between its ends and the posts
- linesmen and service judge are all correctly placed
- his own high chair is in a direct line with the net

He must also see that enough tested shuttles of varied speeds are readily available so that play is continuous, and resist players' attempts to test them again. Having notified the players of any 'faults' or 'lets' over the court, he will supervise the toss-up; allow precisely three minutes for the knock-up; then, from his chair, announce the players and event, He announces visiting players first and all by forenames and surnames, not Mr,

The umpire, from his vantage point in a high chair, must watch every second of play, look out for infringements, and keep and call the correct score.

Mrs, Miss or Ms. Finally he will call 'Love-all! Play!'

During play

With play at last under way the umpire must be prepared for an hour or more of intense concentration with never a stroke or an action missed. He must listen for a shuttle brushing against hair or shirt, or the slurring sound of a 'sling'; watch for the slightest sway of the net disturbed by shorts or skirt brushed against it, or for a racket taking a shuttle a fraction of a second before it crosses the net. He must be ready to call 'Fault!' or 'Let!' instantly and decisively and be equally alert for service in the wrong order or from the wrong court; for a surreptitious squeezing of the shuttle or a racket handle thrust down between the feathers to speed or slow up its flight; or for a fractional double hit. He must never be swayed by spectator opinion or 'advice'.

On occasion he must be prepared to exert his authority, perhaps to dismiss a drowsy linesman; to curb an outburst of temper; to warn against any distracting noise or time wasting. For all that he cannot overrule a linesman or service judge on point of fact. If the former acknowledges he is unsighted, the umpire can make the decision instead. If he too is unsighted, a 'let' is played.

All the time he must call the score accurately and clearly, so that it can be heard by spectators as well as players, and must do it dispassionately without mannerism or dramatization. He must keep the game flowing, never seeking to make himself the centre of attention. The hallmark of a first-class umpire is that players are scarcely aware that he is there.

THE SERVICE JUDGE

The service judge is a specialist 'umpire' but one concerned only with the legality of a player's service. He is sometimes unpopular, for no player likes to be suddenly told that his normal service action is a 'fault' – especially if the service judge has evaded the issue until a crucial point in the game.

The service judge should sit on a low chair in line with the net and opposite the umpire, with whom he should maintain eye contact. Seated thus he is at eye level with the players' serving actions. If one of them is left-handed or has an unusual action that conceals the actual impact, the service judge should

The signals used by the service judge and what they mean.

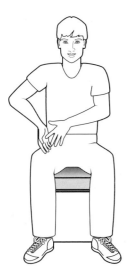

The initial point of contact with the shuttle not on the base of the shuttle.

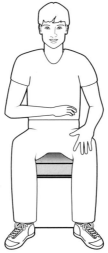

Whole of the shuttle not below the server's waist at point of impact.

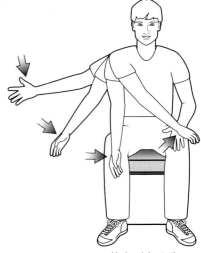

Undue delay to the delivery of the service.

move his base to the other side of the court where a second chair should already have been positioned for just such a situation.

When a player breaks any of the service laws the service judge must call 'Fault!' loudly enough for the player, umpire and the spectators to hear. At the same time he should make the appropriate signal to indicate the type of fault.

If a player does not understand the signal, it must be explained verbally in simple, predetermined phrases. In the rare event of a foreign player still not understanding his fault, the service judge should tell the umpire who can call for the referee, team captain or an interpreter to ensure the least possible delay.

The service judge is also in charge of the reserve supply of shuttles, and hands these to players on request. The players may not test them for speed but may hit them up to verify true flight. If shuttles are changed unnecessarily, he should notify the umpire.

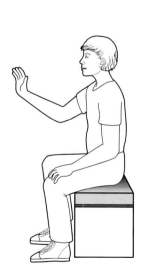

At point of impact the shaft of the racket is not pointing downwards to keep the head of the racket discernibly below the hand holding the racket.

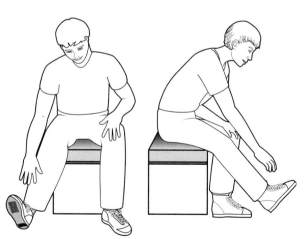

Some part of both feet not in the service court and/or not in a stationary position until the service is delivered.

THE LINESMEN

The linesmen should be seated some 2.5–3.5m (8–12ft) from the court and in prolongation of their designated sideline or service line for which they are entirely responsible. In big matches, over-eager photographers must not be allowed to encroach upon their view or distract them.

Linesmen, like the umpire, must concentrate one hundred per cent. They should not allow themselves to become so involved with the game as an exciting spectacle, or with play on the other side of the court, that they do not clearly see the landing of a shuttle suddenly and sharply angled to their line. Nor must they be tempted to call before a shuttle actually lands; drift has been known to waft a shuttle an extra 300mm (1ft) 'in' or 'out' at the last second! The linesmen's signals are as follows:

- if a shuttle lands 'out', even if it is well out, he must call 'Out!' loudly enough for all to hear and signal by extending his arms horizontally outwards at chest height
- if it is 'in', he remains silent and points downwards at the line with his right hand

The signals used by the linesmen and what they mean.

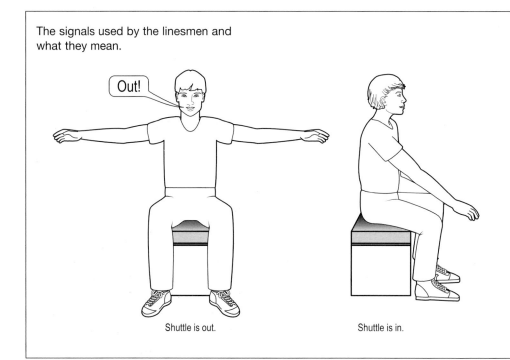

Out!

Shuttle is out.

Shuttle is in.

- if he has been unsighted, he should indicate this by placing both his hands over his eyes

These signals should be maintained for a few seconds so that everyone may see them. An erroneous call can be retracted provided it is done immediately. Linesmen must not yield to silent harassment (hands on hips and an astounded expression!) from a player. If such behaviour occurs, he should report it to the umpire if the latter has not already cautioned or warned the offender

Well-briefed and well-situated, umpire, service judge and linesmen

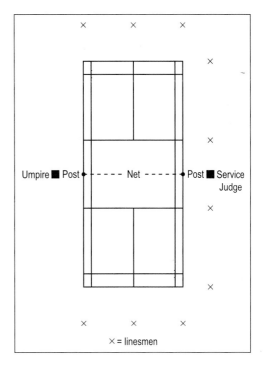

The positions of the umpire, service judge and linesmen around a doubles court.

work as a team. The former should discreetly acknowledge the signals of the two latter. Even in a club tournament, such controls as there are should never be allowed to become sloppy.

Often at this level, however, a stepladder from the caretaker's cupboard has to double for the usual imposing official high chair! Take heart if this is your lot, for even in the prestigious All England Championships in 1912 the umpire was photographed precariously enthroned in this way!

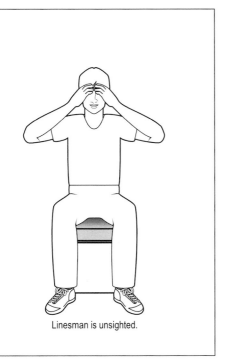

Linesman is unsighted.

RULES CLINIC

If, on winning the toss in doubles, I elect to serve first, shall I also be able to receive first?

Only if you do not score a point or if you score a run of 2, 4, 6 or more even points. Such points will bring you back to the right-hand court.

In mixed doubles I like my partner to move in quickly for a 'kill' off my service. To this end, is she allowed to take up her stance in front of me?

Yes, she may stand where she wishes, in the right-hand or left-hand court, provided she does not in any way block the receiver's sight of the whole of your service and, presumably, does not hamper your action. This formation could also apply to a weak lady in ladies' doubles but would virtually never apply to men's doubles.

When my partner is too busy striking the shuttle to watch the lines, I like to help by calling 'Yes!', 'No!', 'Watch!'. **If I have to call very sharply, can this be construed as 'distraction' by my opponent?**

No. It is a recognized practice. You are not calling when one of your opponents is actually striking, so it cannot be said to be distracting.

If my partner and I, going for the same shot down the centre line, clash rackets but between us hit the shuttle over the net, is this regarded as a 'double hit'?

No, it is a valid stroke as only one racket, the foremost, actually hits the shuttle. This, of course, is provided that the shuttle is cleanly hit and neither slung nor hit twice in succession as a result of the clash.

A mixed doubles partnership showing the woman standing in front of her serving partner, ready to attack the opponents' return. Shuttle and racket are both very near illegality.

If in a third game we forget to change ends with the score at 8, are we then precluded from doing so for the rest of the game?

No. You may change ends as soon as the fault is recognized, and the score stands.

In lungeing to retrieve a very tight drop-shot to the net, can I put my non-racket hand down to help maintain my balance and/or to recover more quickly?

There is no law against this.

In handicap events what is meant by 'owe a hand' or 'give a hand'?

'Owe a hand' means that only you *or* your partner can serve, i.e. you have only one serve, not two, between you. 'Give a hand' means you allow your opponents an extra serve, i.e. three in all. These are crippling handicaps that may even be augmented by 'owe 6' or 'owe 8' as well. Such players are really too good to enter handicap events.

If a player does not return a 'dead' shuttle to his serving opponent until he (the former) has actually returned to his base, is this transgressing the law on 'continuous play'?

No. Provided that the shuttle is then hit immediately and accurately back to the waiting server. It is not an uncommon way to prevent an over-eager opponent serving before the receiver is ready.

If, in serving, my racket hits the base and the feathers at the same time, is this a legal serve?

No. The Laws clearly state that the racket must 'initially hit the base'.

I'm told that some players are so athletic that they jump with both feet off the ground at impact in order to hit harder, earlier and more steeply. Is this permitted?

Yes, it is perfectly legal. Most effective and exciting too! It is only in serving that the Laws insist that both feet, or part of both feet, are in contact with the ground at impact.

In the summer I play badminton in the garden with an outdoor shuttlecock. May I use these indoors as well?

This is not a good idea as, in order to give them some stability against the wind, they are much more heavily weighted than indoor ones. This makes them faster than allowed by the Laws on serving (see page 15). On a smaller, indoor court one of these, well struck, could cause serious facial injury to a player at the net.

If, when I am serving, the shuttle hits the tape and falls short of the front service line, is this a fault? Or am I allowed to play a 'let'?

The serve cannot be replayed if it hits the tape – as in tennis. If it falls short of the front service line, it must be treated as a fault.

I wear glasses when on court. If I play very energetically they sometimes slip off onto the floor. Can I appeal to an opponent or umpire for a 'let' in order to prevent their breakage and to restore my full vision?

Unfortunately, no. Appeal to your optician to tighten the 'arms' of your spectacles; or fix an elastic band to them to go round the back of your head. Or perhaps try contact lenses.

If my glasses mist up so severely that my vision of the shuttle is blurred, can I stop and clean them?

You can – but only a very quick wipe, that does not hold up play, is allowed. Some players unfortunately make this an excuse for a quick breather. It is much better to invest in an absorbent towelling headband and to use glasses demister before you start play.

If, when I serve, the shuttle remains on top of the tape or, after crossing the net, is caught in the mesh, is this a fault?

In service it is. But if this unusual situation occurs in general play a 'let' is played.

As I am relatively short, I rise up on tiptoe when serving to obtain a flatter trajectory. Is that a legal serve?

Yes, indeed, provided part of both feet are in contact with the floor at impact.

If in an away match I find the floor is very slippery, can I apply resin to it or to the soles of my shoes?

Yes, but out of courtesy, you should ask the home club secretary's and team captain's permission.

If a, player is forced to retire by injury during a doubles match, can his partner be allowed a replacement player?

If the injury occurs during play, no. If it happens before play, yes, provided that the substitute has not already played in the event with another partner. The referee should post up a notice to this effect, to allow protests – if any.

If, in serving, I hold the shuttle by the sticky lacquered threads round it, and as a result get an uneven drop, can I leave it and ask for a 'let'?

If you have not commenced your forward swing, yes. If you have, then No, for the serve starts with that first forward swing and must be continuous.

I know that in serving I am not allowed to hit the feathers first. Is it legal, however, to slice across them in a smash or a drop-shot?

Yes, both are legal strokes that deceptively bring the shuttle down more steeply than the receiver anticipates.

Can trainers be worn on a badminton court?

There is no law against this. A local rule however might outlaw heavy ones from the point of view both of looks and of possible damage to the floor covering. They will certainly slow down your essential speed of movement on court.

RANKING

This is an official, international rating of a player's current ability. It is arrived at by a cleverly devised but complicated system administered by the IBF and is too complicated for detailed explanation here. Briefly, however, it is founded on a points system. These points are based on a player's 12 best results in IBF-graded events (except for junior and invitational ones) during the previous 52 weeks. They are awarded on sliding scales according to:

- how far the player progressed in such events
- grading of the event
- time reduction (time elapsed since the result)

The World Championships, Sudirman Cup, Olympic Games, World Grand Prix Finals, and World Cup are the IBF's major events. Along with the Grand Prix tournaments, all have carefully differentiated points.

To these are added bonus points when a player beats one ranked above him at that time: the higher the opponent's ranked position the more points awarded.

Points won (including bonus points) in an event are subject to a time-reduction factor. This means points from events played more than 13 weeks ago become worth 90 per cent of their original value; 26 weeks ago, 75 per cent; 39 weeks ago, 55 per cent.

Points are awarded in the same way for men's, ladies', and mixed doubles – provided there is no change of partner.

The table on page 56 is an example of how a player's points are worked out. The calculations cover only the games that have been played within the previous 52 weeks.

The top 200 players in singles and the top 100 partnerships in doubles are updated weekly on the Fax-u-back system. The top 200 singles and top 100 doubles are distributed monthly, and a full list is sent quarterly. This mammoth worldwide task is efficiently

● NATIONAL AND INTERNATIONAL EVENTS

In the higher echelons there are scores of national championships (at junior age-levels too), restricted to members of that country. There are national open championships, the Nordic Championships, European Championships, Commonwealth Games and, recently, even Mediterranean, Oceania and Balkan Championships. To say nothing of Grand Prix tournaments, continental championships, the World Championships and the Olympic Games – for today badminton ranks with the elite sports and is enjoyed worldwide.

● ENTRY FORMS

For most events entry forms, obtained from the tournament secretary, must be completed, signed, and returned to him. They should detail the following:

- whereabouts of, and routes to, the venue
- timetable of the events being played; the entry fees charged; and the prizes offered: cheques, vouchers and/or trophies

- details of nearest catering, and string repairs
- an instruction to report to the referee immediately on arrival
- a warning that a player not ready to go on court when called may be disqualified at the referee's discretion
- the make of shuttles, feathered or synthetic, to be used
- details of spectator accommodation, charges, and the anticipated finals' starting time
- space for insertion of details of earliest possible arrival times if that is later than the scheduled one

● THE DRAW

Byes
When the number of entrants for a tournament event is to the power of two – 4, 8, 16, 32, 64, and so on – there will follow an orderly progression of players/pairs through the early rounds right on to the quarter-finals, semi-finals and the final itself.

This cannot happen when the number of entrants is not to the power of two – 10, 15, 22, 49, and so on. Byes (dispensations from having to play in the first round) are given to bring the number of players in the second round to a power of 2.

No fewer than seven simultaneous matches taking place in the early stages of the famous All England Championships.

The number of such byes is found by subtracting the actual number of entrants, say 41, from the next highest number to the power of two, in this case 64. This leaves 23 byes, while 18 entrants play the first round.

These byes must if possible be divided equally between the two halves of the draw. Where this is not possible, the extra bye will be placed in the top half. In the top half, all byes are placed at the top of their respective eighths; in the bottom half, at the bottom of their respective eighths.

Seeding

The seeded players are the best players in each event, as selected by the seeding committee which bases its choice on IBF international ranking lists, or more localized ones, or on personal knowledge. Seeding works in the following way:

Up to 15 players	2 seeds
16–31 players	4 seeds
32–63 players	8 seeds
Over 64 players	16 seeds

To prevent 'clashes of the giants' in the early rounds these players are placed, as described below, as far apart as possible. Thus rank and file players have rather more chance of a meeting with a well-known player;

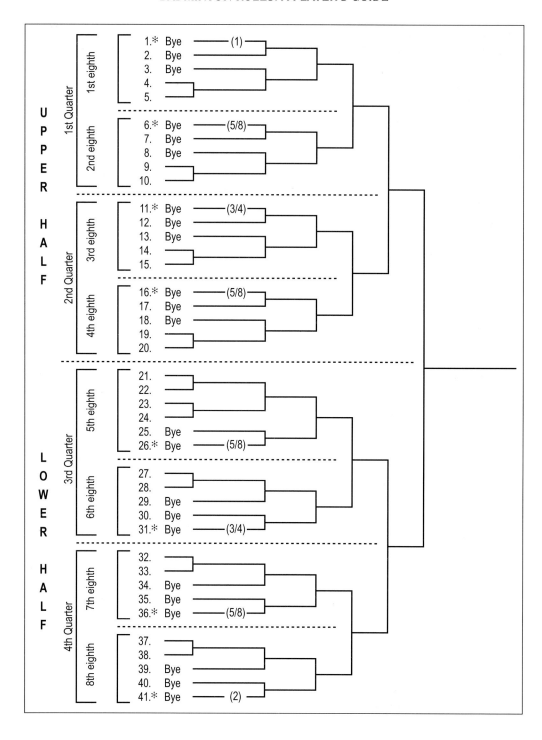

spectators will enjoy more of their skills and, if all runs true to form, the two best players should meet in a well-matched final.

Number one seed is placed at the top of the draw; number two at the bottom. Numbers three and four are drawn by lot to fill the top and bottom slots in the other two quarters. If there are eight seeds, numbers five, six, seven and eight are placed, again by lot, in the remaining eighths. Thus, hopefully, the eight best players will meet in exciting quarter-finals. The table opposite shows an example of a seeded draw.

Details of the positioning of both seeds and byes for every possible entry from 3–64 players can be found in the invaluable BAE *Handbook*.

It has been known for players from a distant country to travel halfway across the world, only to find they have been drawn against each other in the first round! To prevent such occurrences the two top-ranked players may be placed in separate halves, the next two, in the two remaining quarters, and so on. Similar provisions are made to prevent such early clashes between players of the same county.

● TEAM EVENTS

There are world team championships, the Uber Cup and the Thomas Cup, both owing their inception to great English players of the 1920s and 1930s. Sir George Thomas, Bart, winner of a mixed bag of 21 All England titles, inaugurated and gave the Thomas Cup for men's team events (1948–49).

Similarly Betty Uber who between 1926 and 1951 played in 51 international matches – and won the lot – inaugurated and gave the Uber Cup for women's team events (1956–57). Much more recently, in 1989, the Indonesian Badminton Association filled the gap between the two with the Sudirman Cup (named after Indonesia's great player and administrator) for mixed teams.

The All England Championships, the Wimbledon of badminton, beanstalked from a local one-day tournament held at Guildford in 1898 to its present proportions of over 200 entries, many worldwide, for a five-day event at the National Exhibition Centre in Birmingham. It also involves a roughly similar number of court officials and behind-the-scenes helpers.

A clear example of the placement of seeded players and byes in an event involving 41 players. (Courtesy of the BAE)

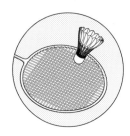

USEFUL ADDRESSES

National Badminton Associations

Australian Badminton Association
PO Box 629
Kew 3101, Victoria
Australia
Tel: +61 3 9819 4300

Badminton Canada
1600 James Naismith Drive
Gloucester
Ontario, K1B 5N4
Canada
Tel: +1 613 748 5605

Badminton Association of the People's
    Republic of China
9 Tiyukuan Road
Beijing 100763
People's Republic of China
Tel: +86 10 6711 8053

Dansk (Danish) Badminton Forbund
Idraettens Hus
Brondby Stadion 20
DK-2605 Brondby
Denmark
Tel: +45 43 262 626

Badminton Association of England Ltd
National Badminton Centre
Bradwell Road
Loughton Lodge
Milton Keynes MK8 9LA
Tel +44 1908 568 822

Deutscher (German) Badminton-
    Verband e.V.
Sudstrasse 25
D-45470 Mulheim a.d. Ruhr
Germany
Tel: +49 208 308 270

Badminton Association of India
D-196 A, Bapunagar
Jaipur 302 015
Rajasthan
India
Tel: +91 141 511 042

Persatuan Bulutangkis Seluruh Indonesia
Jl Damai Raya
Kelurahan Cipayung
Kec. Cipayung
Jakarta-Timur 13840
Indonesia
Tel: +62 21 844 5078/5080